Kids Under Construction

Help for the Strong-Willed Child

F. Russell Crites, Jr.

Published by CPC Dallas, Texas.

Printed in the United States of America

Library of Congress Cataloging-in-publication Data.

Crites, Jr. Floyd Russell

Kids Under Construction: Help for the Strong-Willed Child / F. Russell Crites, Jr.

Psychology / Psychotherapy / Child & Adolescent

ISBN-13: 978-1537678825

ISBN-10: 1537678825

First Edition

The strategies, techniques contained in this workbook are not intended as a substitute for consulting with your mental health provider. In addition, this work is being sold with the understanding that neither the author nor the publisher is engaged in rendering medical, or psychological advice or diagnosis. Neither the author, nor the publisher shall be liable for any loss, injury, or damage allegedly arising from any information or suggestions in this book.

Multiple strategies and information was taken from:

Crites, Jr. F. Russell **Family Therapy Manual: A Pragmatic Approach to Addressing Dysfunctional Family Issues – Revised.** Dallas, TX: CPC, 2016.
Crites, Jr. F. Russell **The Responsibility Factor: High Risk vs Low Risk Parenting.** Being Revised.

Acknowledgement: Some of the worksheets that are in this manual have been a result of information that has been collected over the years. As a result, there is no way in which I can give credit where credit is due. However, I do want to give a general thank you to teachers, all my professors, mentors and fellow therapists who have given me the input necessary to put this workbook together.

For grammatical consistency and clarity, the pronouns "he", "his" and "him" have been used throughout instead of "she or he", "his or her" and "her and him." No sexual bias or insensitivity is intended.

About the Author

F. Russell Crites, Jr. worked for the public schools for over twenty-five years where he did Psychological Testing for a variety of emotional conditions, ADHD, Autism, Learning Issues, etc. He also did behavioral programming for schools and individual students, as well as teacher and parent training for a multitude of issues. Russ has been a consultant for public and private schools, psychiatric hospitals, a variety of agencies, and has had a private practice for over thirty years. In addition, Russ has worked closely with a codependency unit at a local hospital where he provided multiple programs, did groups and individual therapy for people who were seeking treatment. He also helped run an outpatient Drug/Alcohol rehabilitation program where he provided programs, group therapy, individual therapy and assessment for family of origin, codependency and other related issues. Russ currently holds a license as a marriage and family therapist (LMFT), a professional counselor (LPC), and is a licensed specialist in school psychology (LSSP). He also has his clinical membership in the American Association of Marriage and Family Therapy (AAMFT), is a certified clinical Hypnotherapist, is a Certified Professional Coach (CPC) and holds many other certifications. Over the years he has spoken at local, state, regional and national conferences. Topics for some of those conferences or programs were Family of Origin Issues, Codependency, Assessing Family of Origin and Codependency Issues, Marriage & Family, Couple Issues, Parenting, Bipolar Disorder, ADHD, Executive Function Disorders, Depression, Anxiety, Learning Issues, Self-Esteem, and much more. Russ has also provided staff development training for school districts, businesses and other agencies. He is the founder and director of Crites Psycho-Educational Consultants. Russ completed a B.S. in psychology with a minor in Bible and a M.S. in Clinical/Counseling Psychology from Abilene Christian University. He has completed post masters work in Marriage and Family, Counseling and Psychology in order to meet the requirements for additional licenses and certifications.

Table of Contents

Note to Parents

This work is not intended to be a complete guide to parenting. It does not cover many issues that would be addressed if that were the case. The primary intent of this work is to help you identify strategies and a system that will help you better control a child who is out of control in some way. Your child might be oppositional, have conduct issues or he may simply be very strong willed. Regardless of the issue your child has, this work provides tools that will help you manage his behavior in an easier more effective way.

One of the most often seen issues today in many children is entitlement. They believe that they should get things even when they don't deserve them. They also believe that they should be on the receiving end without putting any work into the process of obtaining things. As a result, work ethic has become a thing of the past and children are paying the cost by becoming self-centered, selfish, demanding, irresponsible and yes entitled as was previously stated.

In addition, far too many children often demand to be able to play their computer games and will make their parents miserable if they do not comply. Such children often believe that they have the right to play without being responsible. In some cases, they may even refuse to follow directives unless they get something they want. In addition, such children may refuse to clean their room, put things up, etc. and expect you to be the maid, cook, taxi driver and bottle washer. It's as if many children in today's world believe that they are lord and ruler in the home and parents are to do for them as they decree it.

When this happens, families start to struggle mightily. Parents are frustrated. Kids are out of control. Everything seems to be out of synch and life on a day to day basis becomes even more difficult than normal. If this describes issues that you or your family are experiencing, this work is for you. It is important to note that this system is not meant for children who have disabilities that are causing them to behave inappropriately. When that is the case, there are multiple strategies that would need to be put into place that would specifically address their particular issues. This work does not cover those issues, but can be a supportive tool.

The contents and aids within this work will help you do what is needed to help your child become the person you want him to be. Each section is important and provides you with a piece to the puzzle so that you can help your child. It is important that you completely read and work through each section and understand how to use the information being suggested. If you leave out any part of this system it could very likely cause you to be less successful.

Good Luck on your Journey

F. Russell Crites, Jr.

8

COMMUNICATION AND DISCIPLINE

This section provides you with basic communication tools that you should or should not be using. It's important that you learn how to communicate in ways that will be clear to your child and simple for you. Parents often over-communicate when trying to discipline. Keep it simple. It will reduce your stress and put the pressure on your child to make the right decision or accept the consequences. You just need to use good communication and provide adequate consequences in order to hold him accountable for his actions.

- Communication 101: When Disciplining a Child
- Ineffective Passive Communication
- Assertive Communication
- Ineffective Aggressive Communication
- Developing Assertive Communication Messages
- Three Magic Words
- Using EIAG After a Poor Choice

Communication 101
When Disciplining a Child

Key Rules for Communication and Discipline:

Do Not

- Do not raise your voice.
- Do not get angry, yell or try to be more powerful.
- Do not threaten with body language.
- Do not continue to discuss what has happened.
- Do not add consequence upon consequence when in the middle of severe outburst or serious opposition.
- Do not discuss the event when a bad decision is made. If he wants to discuss it, do it after the consequence has been completed.
- During an 'event' do not get into a discussion about what is fair or not fair after you have identified consequences. Walk away….provide additional consequences if he continues.

Do

- Do be calm.
- Do be soft spoken.
- Do **express empathy** for their loss of privilege, toy, phone, computer, etc.
- Do add an additional consequence if he does not comply (It's your choice).
- The additional consequence will most often be, "You will not be able to do anything you want to do, touch any toy, listen to music, until you complete the initial consequence. It's your choice."
- Discuss how your child could have handled it better (See EIAG) when he is calmed down. Give him time.
- Do show your **love and concern** verbally.
- Do **verbalize valued foundational beliefs** that help the child learn good Self-Judgment
- Do verbalize your joy, pleasure, thanks, etc. when he makes a good choice (Self-Discipline).
- Always….Always…. Say, "**It's your Choice."** You simply let him know what the consequence will be if he makes the wrong choice (This should be done in advance as much as is possible—See Behavior = Consequences chart). This allows him to make a decision (Self-Discipline) based on two things. First, he must think about the values you have taught. Will this decision go against or go along with those values (this is self-judgment at work). Second, he must decide if in making the wrong decision is it worth the consequence that will occur (if he makes the wrong decision more than once in a short period of time you may need to make the consequence stronger. However, it's still his choice.
- Do verbalize that if he does not accept the consequence a more severe consequence will occur.
- REMEMBER: YOU CAN'T MAKE YOUR CHILD DO ANYTHING. Initially, your job is to provide positive reinforcers (that should be gradually phased out over time), teach values with love, provide him with opportunities to utilize self-discipline and provide consequences if he makes wrong choices. The more often he makes correct self-disciplined decisions, the more responsible he becomes. Regardless, it's still his choice!!!

Ineffective Passive Communication

Ineffective communication has no place in your parent-child communications if you want to train up healthy, responsible children. The first ineffective communication occurs when we are to passive. Passive Communication is made up of vague, unclear, non-assertive statements. When a parent uses this type of communication it suggests to a child that,

      1) you don't mean what you say, and/or

      2) you are not ready or willing to take any action.

When this occurs, your child will most often test you until you finally take a firm stand. There are five basic types of non-assertive responses addressed here. None of these are truly effective. They are as follows:

NON-ASSERTIVE RESPONSES

1. Questioning   "Just what do you think you're doing, young man?"

2. Begging and Pleading   "Would you please behave."

3. Stating Facts   "You are not minding me again."

4. Assertive statement   "If you don't stop that right now you with no follow through will go to your bedroom (doesn't follow through)."

5. Ignoring the Problem   Maybe, if I just ignore it, he won't do it anymore.

THOUGHT QUESTION

Do you believe you do any of the above? If so, if so go to the next page!

Ineffective Passive Communication

Worksheet

Put a check mark next to the ineffective communication methods you use. List up to three examples that communicate how you have used any of the ineffective communication methods. How effective were they?

____Questioning

"Just what do you think you're doing young man?"

_____

_____

How has your child taken advantage of things when you use this ineffective communication method?

____Begging and Pleading

"Would you please behave."

_____

_____

How has your child taken advantage of things when you use this ineffective communication method?

____Stating Facts

"You are not minding me again."

_____

_____

How has your child taken advantage of things when you use this ineffective communication method?

____Assertive statement with no follow-through

"Put your toys up or go to your room (no follow through)."

_____

_____

How has your child taken advantage of things when you use this ineffective communication method?

____Ignoring the Problem

(Maybe if I just ignore it he won't do it anymore.)

_____

_____

How has your child taken advantage of things when you use this ineffective communication method?

Write a brief statement saying why you are committed to not use ineffective passive communication with your child from this point forward.

Ineffective Aggressive Communication

Aggressive Communication often communicates a hostile, critical attitude that often ridicules, tears down, tells ways to fail and negates positive feelings. Aggressive Communication tends to suggest to children that you don't care about their feelings or needs. The problem with the aggressive communication style is that it seems to be so effective. However, the effectiveness of hostile, aggressive communication is usually short lived and produces rebellion and/or fear in children. The following is a short list of obvious verbal aggression examples.

VERBAL AGGRESSION

- "I can't believe you're so stupid."

- "You're acting like a retard."

- "You make me sick."

- "You're pretty smart for a dummy."

- "We should have adopted."

- "We never wanted you."

- "You are a bad child."

- "If you do that again I'm going to beat you black and blue."

- "You will never go to the movie again if you are not careful."

- "If you do that again I'll slap you silly."

- "I'll spank you until you can't walk."

- Using disrespectful language.

- Using foul language with your child.

Do you use any form of verbal aggression? It doesn't have to be listed above. If you do, write it down below. Keep in mind that if you use this form of communication you are probably alienating your child and damaging your relationship. This often produces rebellious behavior.

Personal Example:

Write a brief statement saying why you are committed to not use ineffective aggressive communication with your child from this point forward.

Assertive Communication

Assertive Communication is firm, fair, consistent and positive in orientation. It provides parents with the communication tools that are necessary if one is to correct children in a way that will provide responsibility building situations.

RULES FOR SPEAKING ASSERTIVELY

RULE #1: DON'T SEND "M AND M'S" (MIXED MESSAGES)

If you are going to tell someone to not do something, then you should not be doing it yourself. If you are then you are sending mixed messages. Children do what they see more than what they are told.

RULE #2: BODY LANGUAGE SHOULD BE CONSISTENT WITH YOUR WORDS.

When you communicate make sure that your body language is communicating similar messages.

For instance:

Verbal	**Body Language**
You are being stern	Show disappointment on your face
You are unhappy with a choice your child has made.	May frown or shake your head in a negative way.

RULE #3: ALWAYS REMAIN CALM WHEN YOU COMMUNICATE!

If you can remain calm when you talk to your child you will be much more effective as you deal with him. Children can sense anger or other feelings and will often respond to them instead of what you are saying verbally.

RULE #4: YOU MUST BE SPECIFIC!

If you are to communicate about a problem, you must be very specific when you tell your child something. Do not speak in generalities.

Don't	**Do**
"I need you to pick up things in your room."	"I need you to pick up your toys and put them where they belong."
"Stop that!"	"Stop poking your sister in the side."

Personal Examples:

Give two personal examples of how you might be too general when you are trying to correct behavior. After you identify your example rewrite it and be more specific.

      Example One:

      Restate using specifics:

      Example Two:

      Restate using specifics:

Developing Assertive Communication Messages

Please list five additional assertive messages for each of the four areas shown. What would be five situations that might call for you to be assertive. Let these situations be your guide as you develop your assertive messages.

Teaching

"You should always clean up the bathroom when you are finished. Just as a reminder clean up means, sink cleaned out, counter wiped off and everything put back in proper place, dirty clothes in hamper, and towel put back where it belongs."

_____

_____

_____

_____

_____

Moral Development

"It's important that you never lie to anyone."

_____

_____

_____

_____

_____

Directing

"You need to be ready to leave for school by 7:30 AM."

_____

_____

_____

_____

_____

Warning

"Stop poking your sister or you will go to your room."

_____

_____

_____

_____

_____

Three Magic Words

"It's Your Choice."

The most important words after "I love you" are, "It's your choice." Parents say, "I can't let him decide, he won't do the right thing." That's the point. It is up to him to make the right or wrong choice. If he makes the right choice you can praise him for the right choice, encourage him to continue to make right choices, and show your appreciation. Each time he makes an appropriate choice he becomes a bit more responsible. If he makes the wrong choice you give him a predetermined consequence. That's poor self-discipline. If he keeps making a specific wrong choice, you should increase the consequence. Ultimately, he will comply….even if he doesn't like it. However, it's still his choice. This reduces your workload and puts the responsibility back on your child to make good choices or accept the consequences. Your job is mostly done once you identify the problem behaviors and the consequences that will occur when inappropriate choices are made.

Consider the following:

- **Say it every time:** Consistency is extremely important. That means every time he is in a position to make a choice say, **"It's Your Choice".**
- Use a soft, low voice. **Don't raise your voice and don't argue.**
- Say it once and let him make his choice.
- **Remind him of the consequence** (if he has not already broken the rule or exhibited the inappropriate behavior).
- If he makes a bad choice **don't discuss it**. Simply give him the consequence. You **should** discuss it later when the consequence has been completed (Use EIAG).
- *If the consequence is a time out and he refuses to comply, remind him that he will not be able to do anything else until it is complete. Anything he touches is taken away and he must earn it back before he can touch it again. Again say, "It's your choice."*
- Don't stand there and let a child yell, argue or talk to you inappropriately. You can walk away. However, if he uses words or says something inappropriate he should receive a predetermined consequence.
- Keep the rules and consequences that you establish in this system posted so you can review them. It will help you deal with his specific issues. They should always keep these posted until things are much better.
- **Be sad, empathetic** that he has 'lost' a privilege, toy, etc. "I'm sorry you lost…..I know that it was something that you enjoy." No need to get mad, say you deserve it. Be sad he made a bad choice, but make sure he knows it was his choice, not yours.

Buy Back Rule: Earning back is an important aspect of this system. If a child loses an object or privilege he must earn it back through chores. He cannot use money that he has in the bank or in his piggy bank, etc. to pay for it. He may not use the item or privilege until it is earned back. Yes, he can choose to not earn it back. You simply remove it, or make it something he cannot access until he chooses to earn it back.

Using EIAG After a Poor Choice

Exploring is one of the most important tools you can use to help a child learn how to make better choices in the future. After the event, after your child has calmed down, and after the consequence have completed, take a moment and do EIAG. All inappropriate behavior can be used as an opportunity to teach your child more appropriate behavior, clarify your values or beliefs and generally teach your child what your expectations are for him. When you ask the What? Why? and How? questions you are helping your child clarify what is right, what is wrong and how he can handle things better in the future. Make copies of this worksheet (see appendices). You can use it over and over as you help your child learn how to identify better choices.

E.I.A.G.: EXPERIENCE-IDENTIFY-ANALYZE-GENERALIZE		
Steps	Questions to Ask	Personal Example
Experience:	Something Happens	
Identify:	Ask: "What happened?" "What are you feeling?" "What did you see?"	
Analyze:	Ask: "Why was that significant?" "What caused that to happen?" "Why did it happen to you?" "What made that important?"	
Generalize:	Ask: "How can you use this?" "How could you do it differently next time?" "What did you learn from the experience?"	

Adapted from Steven Glenn's work entitled, Raising Self-Reliant Children in a Self-Indulgent World.

NOTES PAGE:

STRATEGIES TO REDUCE INAPPROPRIATE OR UNWANTED BEHAVIORS

If you can identify and redirect a child's behavior just before it becomes a problem you can reduce conflict significantly. Strategy wise this is one of your first lines of defense in dealing with behavioral issues. The more effective you are with this, the easier your life will be. Read each of the strategies below and pick one or two that you will try.

- **The Great Diversion**
- **Request Desirable Behavior**
- **Relocate Your Child**
- **Make Substitutions**
- **Distraction**

The Great Diversion

Diversion is not like other disciplinary techniques. It calls for the parent to learn the subtle art of re-direction. This simply means that you refocus your child's attention on to some other object, activity, etc. to get him to stop a certain behavior.

Instructions

1. Identify two situations that are often a problem with your child at home or when you are out. Write them in the space provided below.
2. Think about the situation and come up with a statement that can be used to redirect your child in order to avoid a conflict.

Situation #1

_____

_____

_____

_____

Diversion for Situation #1

_____

_____

Situation #2

_____

_____

_____

_____

Diversion for Situation #2

_____

_____

Specific Quick Redirections

Request Desirable Behavior

Focus: Change an inappropriate behavior to an appropriate behavior, i.e., replace throwing rocks (inappropriate) with throwing balls (appropriate).

Redirection is often much more successful than telling your child to stop doing something. When you redirect you should be very specific about what you want your child to do. For example: If your child is running don't say, "Stop running." Proper redirection would be, "You need to walk when you are in the house."

Substitutions

Focus: Alleviate issues through substitution.

Substitutions are also another good form of redirection. If your child sees another child playing with something, inevitably he will want to play with it also. Substitution calls for you identify something else that will get his attention. It might be another toy, or possibility even time with you (reading, talking, looking at other things, etc.) in order to get his attention off the other child's toy.

Relocation

Focus: Change behavior by removing child from the situation.

Relocation is another very helpful tool. If your child is exhibiting a behavior that is unacceptable, dangerous, irritating to others, etc. you can use relocation. For instance, if he is irritating other children who are trying to swing at the park, simply walk him over to the monkey bars and say you want to see if he can climb to the top.

Distraction

Focus: Distracting your child from the event or situation that is causing him distress or that is causing a problem of some kind. Distraction is especially useful with younger children or babies. However, it can be adapted to be used with other children.

The purpose of distraction is simply to get your child's mind off of the situation that is causing him to be upset without redirecting him. You may make faces, shake a rattle, or play with a toy he likes while he is watching you. You are not trying to redirect. You are simply doing something that gets his attention and hopefully causes him to forget what it was that was causing him some distress.

DISCIPLINARY CONSEQUENCES

Consequences are one of the keys to teaching a child how to behave appropriately. Without consequences children will often develop unwanted behaviors and cause ongoing problems for parents. This section is important. It will be a resource for you when you start identifying the consequences you will use for your child in a later section. Read this section well and pay specific attention to the 'Guidelines for Using Consequences' page.

- **Possible Disciplinary Consequences**
  - ➤ **Natural Consequences**
  - ➤ **Logical Consequences**
  - ➤ **Removal of Privileges**
  - ➤ **Time Out**
  - ➤ **Isolation**
  - ➤ **Grounding**
  - ➤ **Corporal Punishment**
- **Guidelines for Using Consequences**

Possible Disciplinary Consequences

There are many disciplinary strategies that can be used by parents when their child is misbehaving. Some of these are listed below:

NATURAL CONSEQUENCES

A Natural consequence is a consequence that occurs when you allow the child to experience a negative consequence that occurs naturally without your aid. For instance, if a child goes outside without a coat and it is cold he gets cold, it he goes out without an umbrella he gets rained on, etc.

LOGICAL CONSEQUENCES

Logical consequences are consequences that occur that relates directly to the inappropriate behavior in some way. Two examples of logical consequences are as follows:

Your young child fails to put up toys! The logical consequence would be that he would not be allowed to play with them the next day.

Your teenager comes in late Friday night! The logical consequence would be that he would not be allowed to go out next Friday night!

REMOVAL OF PRIVILAGES

Loss of privileges is a method that calls for the parent to take away their children's favorite toys, T.V., phone or other special items or privileges as a disciplinary measure. Determine what is special to your child and take away those things when he needs to be disciplined.

TIME OUT

Time out is a method in which the child is put in a situation where, for a specific amount of time, he must remain quiet and not participate in any activities. He can watch other people having fun or doing things with the family, but he may not participate until the time-out is over.

ISOLATION

Isolation is a powerful method to change behavior. He should be placed in a location where he cannot make contact with anyone else visually. The bedroom (preferably in the middle of the bed) is one very good place for isolation. When he is sitting on the bed he must not play with a toy, listen to music, watch T.V. or do anything else. He must sit in the middle of the bed and do nothing. He may not lie down or get up without permission. If he touches a toy, or uses anything in his room it is to be taken away for two days to a week. If he tries to leave his room you may choose to give him one swat, put him in isolation for 15 minutes the next night for each time he comes out or do whatever else is necessary to get his attention. (To be fair you should explain that there will be further consequences if he does not cooperate with his isolation.)

GROUNDING

Grounding is a method of discipline that calls for the specific restriction of your child to their house or yard for a specified amount of time. Grounding should have a designated amount of time and is usually for longer periods of time than most other disciplinary actions. It should be used sparingly so that it will have a greater effect when it is used. Don't make it too long or the child will often give up hope and you lose the benefit of grounding. It should also be used for more serious inappropriate behaviors.

CORPORAL PUNISHMENT

Corporal punishment, usually in the form of spanking, is not recommended by many professionals. However, there are still a great number of people who use this as a method of discipline. If this is to be used, it should be a last choice and not used often or it loses its effectiveness.

Natural Consequences

Natural consequences occur when you allow the child to experience a consequence that occurs naturally without your aid. For instance, if a child goes outside without a coat and it is cold he gets cold, it he goes out without an umbrella he gets rained on, he gets wet, etc. You must allow the consequence to occur. You can warn, but not force the child to make the right choice. List some examples below that would call for a parent to allow a natural consequence to occur so that the child can learn to be responsible for himself.

General Events   **Consequence**

Events Specific to Your Child   **Consequence**

When you allow your child to experience the consequences that come from bad choices, you give him the opportunity to learn how to make better choices and become more responsible.

Logical Consequences

Logical consequences occur when you tie in a consequence that relates directly to the inappropriate behavior. Some examples of this are listed below for both younger children and for adolescents. In the spaces provided at the bottom of this worksheet list some specific behavior problems and determine what the logical consequence might be.

BEHAVIOR	LOGICAL CONSEQUENCE
Fails to put up toys	Cannot use them the next day
Comes in late Friday night	Cannot go out next Friday night
Fails to clean room	Stays in room until it's clean
Chores not completed	Cannot go out until finished
Child won't do homework	Cannot play until finished
Phone privileges abused	Phone taken away for a day
Throws a toy truck	Loses toy truck for 48 hours

_____   _____

_____   _____

_____   _____

_____   _____

_____   _____

_____   _____

_____   _____

Buy Back Rule: Remind the child of the buyback rule. If you lose something you must buy it back by doing chores before he can get it back.

Removal of Privileges

Loss of privileges is a method that calls for the parent to take away their children's favorite toys, T.V., phone or other special items or privileges as a disciplinary measure. Determine what is special to your child and take away those things when he needs to be disciplined. It does not have to be related to the inappropriate behavior.

List some Privileges that could be taken away from your child! Be specific!!! Keep in mind his activities, toys, electronics, social privileges, etc.

Buy Back Rule: Remind the child of the buyback rule. If you lose something you must buy it back by doing chores before he can get it back.

Time Out

Time out is a method in which the child is put in a situation where, for a specific amount of time, he must remain quiet and not participate in any activities. He can watch other people having fun or doing things with the family, but he may not participate until the time-out is over.

_____

List some examples of how you might use time out with your child! What would time out look like for your child? Where would you put him for time out?

Isolation

Isolation is a method where you place a child in a location where he cannot make contact with anyone else visually. The bedroom (preferably in the middle of the bed) is one very good place for isolation. When he is sitting on the bed he must not play with a toy, listen to music, watch T.V. or do anything else. He must sit in the middle of the bed and do nothing. He may not lie down or get up without permission. If he touches a toy, or uses anything in his room it is to be taken away for two days to a week. If he tries to leave his room you may put him in isolation for 15 minutes the next night for each time he comes out or do whatever else is necessary to get his attention. (To be fair you should explain that there will be further consequences if he does not cooperate with his isolation.)

List some examples of how you might use isolation with your child! What would it look like for your child? Where would he go?

Grounding

Grounding is a method of discipline that calls for the specific restriction of your child to their house or yard for a specified amount of time. Grounding should be limited to two to three days at the most. Longer periods of time cause some children to give up hope and you lose the benefit of the consequence. Some children can tolerate longer times. You must determine what works for you child and what does not work.

Under what circumstances would you use grounding? List them. This should be used for more severe behaviors. Define exactly what grounding would mean if it occurred for your child.

Corporal Punishment

Research

In a large-scale meta-analysis of 88 studies a number of important pieces of data were identified in regards to corporal punishment (Elizabeth Thompson Gershoff, PhD, of the National Center for Children in Poverty at Columbia University). Not everyone agrees with these conclusions. Regardless, if you want you can find the study and read for yourself. There is much more information in the study than is shown below.

- Corporal punishment leads to more immediate compliant behavior in children, but is also associated with physical abuse.
- Gershoff also cautions that her findings do not imply that all children who experience corporal punishment turn out to be aggressive or delinquent. A variety of situational factors, such as the parent/child relationship, can moderate the effects of corporal punishment.
- The meta-analysis also demonstrates that the frequency and severity of the corporal punishment matters. The more often or more harshly a child was hit, the more likely they are to be aggressive or to have mental health problems.

Dr. Diane Baumrind, noted researcher, suggest that parents who use appropriate corporal punishment should be allowed to do so. "The fact that some parents punish excessively and unwisely is not an argument, however, for counseling all parents not to punish at all." She supports the occasional use of spanking as a form of discipline. She states that her research has shown no negative long-term impact on children if the punishment is delivered within an authoritative style where the child does not perceive the action as harsh or cruel. Her findings appear to be supported by Dr. Larzelere, Sather PR, Schneider WN, Larson DB, and Pike.

You can also find research from all the authors mentioned above. Read them if you like to make your own determination.

Conclusion

If corporal punishment is your first method for disciplining your child, it is not appropriate. You should be using a variety of other strategies before you get to the point that corporal punishment is used. Most parents quickly find out that when other disciplinary methods are used appropriately corporal punishment is rarely if ever needed. If it is used it should be used sparingly and appropriately.

If you chose to use corporal punishment, what would be the behaviors that would warrant this consequence?

Guidelines for Using Consequences

There are eight specific guidelines that are extremely important if you are to effectively use consequences with a child.

Instructions:

1. As you read the statements put a check next to the guidelines that you feel you may not be doing as well as you should for your child's benefit.
2. As you read each guideline, write down what you think needs to happen in order for each of these guidelines to be used more effectively from here on out.

_____ 1. Be consistent!

_____ 2. Be calm and provide the consequences.

_____ 3. Be specific!

_____ 4. Provide consequences as soon as possible.

_____ 5. Consequence must be negative to the child.

_____ 6. Make sure your child knows the consequence for behavior in advance (as much as is possible).

_____ 7. Consequences provided as a choice.

_____ 8. Use consequences that work!

BASIC DISCIPLINARY STRATEGIES

These strategies can be used along with the Kid's Under Construction System. They are most useful in helping you guide your child towards a behavior you desire him to exhibit.

- **The Premack Principle:** Helps encourage wanted positive behavior.
- **GWIC or Guess Who's in Charge:** Causes the child to do something he needs to do before he can do something he wants to do.
- **The Broken Record:** Lets the child know that he needs to do something along with a time limitation. A consequence can be suggested if follow up is needed.
- **The Stopper:** Lets the child know he needs to do something. However, he responds back in an inappropriate way. An immediate consequence occurs and you also tell him that he must do what you are requesting or an additional consequence will be given if he does not comply. Always tell him what the second consequence will be.
- **The Victory Technique:** A silent, visual cue that tells a child that he needs to stop a behavior. Consequences are identified in advance.
- **The 321 Technique:** A verbal statement telling the child he has to comply before you count down to one or there is a prearranged consequence that will occur.
- **Look and Tell Technique**
- **Simple Choice technique**
- **Physical Action Technique**

40

The Premack Principle

This principle states that high frequency behaviors can be used as reinforcers for low frequency behaviors. In other words, if you can find a behavior that a child enjoys and exhibits often, you can tie it to a behavior that you want him to increase.

Example: Little boy loves to play with computer game at home, but doesn't like to read.

Mom: "Johnny, you must read five pages in your book and then tell me what you have read before you can play with your computer this evening."

YOUR CHILD'S POSITIVE HIGH FREQUENCY BEHAVIORS

_____

_____

_____

_____

_____

YOUR CHILD BEHAVIORS YOU WANT TO INCREASE

_____

_____

_____

_____

_____

PREMACK STATEMENT FOR ONE AREA OF CONCERN

_____

_____

_____

GWIC or Guess Who's in Charge

The GWIC technique calls for you to have your child finish an undone task before he/she can do what he/she wants to do, e.g., go to visit a friend, or out to play, etc. this is a technique that is used only when minor problems are occurring.

Example of GWIC:

CHILD: "May I go to visit Bobby next door?"

PARENT: "Yes you may, as soon as you finish cleaning your room."

ACTIVITY

List four situations where you could use GWIC with your child and identify a GWIC statement that you would use next time this situation comes up.

1. _____

GWIC Statement:

2. _____

GWIC Statement:

3. _____

GWIC Statement:

4. _____

GWIC Statement:

The Broken Record

The Broken Record is powerful technique that calls for the parent to request a behavior change no more than two (2) times or a consequence occurs. You simply make the same request the second time and add a consequence to it if the child does not comply in the time required. You should keep the following guidelines in mind when you use the Broken Record.

GUIDELINES:

1. Stay calm and be specific.
2. Tell your child what he should or should not do.
3. If he does not comply in a reasonable amount of time you:
   a. make your statement again, but add a consequence for non-compliance, and
   b. a time limitation (must be completed immediately, by 8:00 or before dinner, bed time, etc.)
4. That he has a choice of doing what he has been told to do or he may take the consequence.

WHEN TO USE THE BROKEN RECORD

The Broken Record can be used any time you need your child to do something, e.g., pick up toys, put his clothes up for you after they are washed, take a shower before bedtime, brush teeth.

Example of the Broken Record:

Dad: "Michael, I want you to pick up your toys, it's time for bed."

Child: "Ok, I'll get it done."

Pre-established Rules in Effect:

> Established RULE: Bedtime is 8:00 PM on school nights.
> Buy Back Rule: If you lose a toy, privilege, etc. 1) you lose it for two days, and 2) you must buy it back by doing chores.

Ten minutes later dad walks in and the child only has five more minutes before he must be in bed. Bedtime is 8:00 PM and it is 7:55 PM. Toys are still on the floor and he has not stopped playing

Dad: (Walks up to child, puts hand on shoulder, puts on a serious face
        and looks him in the eye.)

        "You have until 8:00 PM on the dot to pick up your toys, put them where they belong, and be in bed or you will lose them for 48 hours. It's your choice."

Buy Back Rule: Remind the child of the buyback rule. If you lose something you must buy it back by doing chores before he can get it back.

The Stopper

The Stopper calls for an immediate consequence coupled with a statement calling for a parental request to be completed or another consequence will occur.

GUIDELINES:

1. Stay calm and be specific.
2. Give the child an immediate consequence (keep buy back rule in mind)
3. Tell your child what he should or should not do.
4. If he does not comply in a reasonable amount of time you:
   a. make your statement again, but add a consequence for non-compliance, and
   b. a time limitation (must be completed immediately, or by 8:00 or before dinner, bed time, etc.)
5. That he has a choice of doing what he has been told to do or he may take the consequence.

WHEN TO USE THE STOPPER

The Stopper should be used when your child responds to your request in an inappropriate, disrespectful way.

Example of the Stopper:

Dad: "Michael, I want you to pick up your toys, it's time for bed."

Child: "I don't want to and you can't make me."

Dad: (Walks up to child, puts hand on shoulder, puts on a serious face
        and looks him in the eye.)
        "You have just your computer privileges for 48 hours."

        Dad Immediately adds: "You have until 8:00 PM on the dot to pick up your toys, put them where
        they belong, and be in bed or you will lose them for 48 hours also. It's your choice."

Buy Back Rule: Remind the child of the buyback rule. If you lose something you must buy it back by
                    doing chores before he can get it back.

The Victory Technique

The VICTORY technique is a silent technique that you implement by raising three fingers on one hand. The first finger raised is a warning that communicates that your child's behavior is unacceptable or heading towards being unacceptable. The second finger means that he has just received a previously agreed upon discipline. The third finger means that a more severe, longer lasting consequence has just been given. No verbal communication is necessary. An example of the Victory technique is as follows:

Step One: Get your child's attention!

Step Two: Look at your hand, close it and put one finger out for your child to see. This first finger is a warning to stop whatever behavior is being exhibited immediately. If the behavior stops no disciplinary consequence will occur.

Step Three: If the child doesn't stop, make sure that he is looking at you and put your second finger out on your hand. This automatically means that your child is going to receive the consequence that has been prearranged.

Step Four: If you must put a third finger out he will not only have that consequence, but he will also have a more severe consequence occur that will be more long lasting in duration. This should also be prearranged with the child.

321 adaptation of the Victory Technique

The 321 technique is useful for younger children. It has been used for years by parents to help control behavior and increase compliance with their younger children. Any counting technique can work. You may choose to use 1-5, or 1-3 depending on the situation. It can be used with older children also.

- Simply communicate with the child that when you count backwards it means that he is not complying or doing something he shouldn't.
- He has until the count of 1 or he will **receive a consequence that has been prearranged.**
- Make sure he knows what the consequence will be before you use this technique.

Buy Back Rule: Earning back is an important aspect of this system. If a child loses an object or privilege he must earn it back through chores. He cannot use money that he has in the bank or in his piggy bank, etc. to pay for it. He may not use the item or privilege until it is earned back. Yes, he can choose to not earn it back. You simply remove it, or make it something he cannot access until he chooses to earn it back.

Additional Techniques:

Look and Tell: Look and tell is simply what it says. If your child does something wrong do the following:

Parent: Bend down to his eye level, look him in the eyes, and say, "Honey (your choice of word), "What did you do that you know was wrong?"

Option One: Positive Response

   Child: "I took the toy my sister was playing with."
   Parent: "OK. Was that the right thing to do?"
   Child: "No, mommy."
   Parent: "So what should you do right now. Remember, if you do the right thing everything will be alright. If you make the wrong choice there will be a consequence."
   Child: Looks at toy, grimaces and says, "I should give it back to her right now."
   Parent: "Good Choice. Now go do what you said you would do."
   If he gives it back reinforce that he is making a good choice. If not, he gets the consequence.

Option Two: Negative Response

   Child: "Noting, it was my toy she can't play with it."
   Parent: "OK. Was that the right thing to do since you weren't playing with it?"
   Child: "She can't touch my toys. They are mine."
   Parent: "We have talked about sharing right? You know that it's ok for each of you to play with the others toys. Especially if you are not playing with it at the moment. You need to give it back to her right now or you will have a time out (your choice of an age appropriate consequence). It's your choice."

   Child First Scenario: Child gives the toy back and says, "I'm sorry."
   Parent says, "Good choice honey."   All is well!

   Child Second Scenario: Child refuses to give the toy back
   Parent says, "Ok. You have decided to have a time out. You will also lose the privilege of using that toy for two days (the rest of the night, three days, etc.)." NOTE: You may also use the Buy Back concept. This always makes consequences more 'real and meaningful' to a child.

Simple Techniques to help get a child started on a task, etc.

Simple Choice technique: If he has difficulty getting started simply ask him which tool he would like you to give him so he can get started.   For instance, if he supposed to help clean the counter you could say, "Do you want to start by wiping this side of the counter (show him the cleaning towel) or would you rather put the dirty dishes in the dishwasher fist (you can open the dishwasher).

Physical Action Technique: When the child is faced with a task and it seems like he can't get started, ask him to do one small thing that would begin the task. For instance, if he is supposed to mop the kitchen floor for you simply say, "Go get the mop for me." Once he has it, you can point to where you want him to begin.

IDENTIFYING REWARDS AND MOTIVATION

Reinforcers are most effective with younger children. However, when a child is out of control reinforcers can be used at any age to help with modifying behavior. The goal is to use them until the behavior(s) improve. At that point in time you gradually phase out reinforcers you are using. Here are some tools you can use to identify the reinforcers your child may respond best to in order to help modify or improve behavior.

- Home Reinforcement Survey
- Sample Reinforcers
- Tangible and Consumable Reinforcers
- Activity and Adult Approval Reinforcers
- Peer Approval and Other Reinforcers

Home Reinforcement Survey

Name:_____ Grade:____ Teacher:_____ Date:_____

Instructions: Read the following to the child/adolescent and have him pick between the two choices. Place a check mark next to the statement he chooses. He can only pick one of the two statements for each number.

Out of the two items I will name, which would you like to have the most,	Consumable	Tangible	Activity	Adult Approval	Peer Approval
1.) To have your parents tell you that you did something well (Adult Approval) or				❑	
To be given your favorite candy bar (Consumable)	❑				
2.) To receive a book or game you can enjoy (Tangible or		❑			
To be picked by others to be on their team (Peer Approval)					❑
3.) To be given your favorite drink, e.g., soft drink, sports drink (Consumable) or	❑				
To pick a movie to watch at home (Activity)				❑	
4.) To have friends ask you to do something with them (Peer Approval) or					❑
To be given your favorite candy bar (Consumable)	❑				
5.) To have your parents tell others how proud they are of you (Adult Approval) or				❑	
To be picked by others to be on their team (Peer Approval)					❑
6.) To receive a book or game you can enjoy (Tangible)		❑			
Teacher puts a smiley face or says good job on your paper (Adult Approval)				❑	
7.) To be able to go to a restaurant of my choice (consumable) or	❑				
To go to a movie of my choice (Activity)			❑		
8.) To have your teacher tell you how proud she is of you (Adult Approval) or				❑	
To have your favorite meal at home (Consumable)	❑				
9.) To be given your favorite bag of chips (Consumable) or	❑				
To have friends ask you to sit with them (Peer Approval)					❑
10.) To play a game of your choice at home (Activity) or			❑		
To have your teacher tell you how proud she is of you (Adult Approval)				❑	
11.) To pick a movie to watch at home (Activity) or			❑		
To be given a game you can play with (Tangible)		❑			
12.) To be picked by others to be on their team (Peer Approval)					❑
To play a game of your choice (Activity)			❑		
13.) To be given art materials to use (Tangible) or		❑			
To be given your favorite candy bar (Consumable)	❑				
14.) To receive a gift/toy of my choice valued $3.00 or under (Tangible) or		❑			
To have your friends ask you to be leader in a game (Peer Approval)					❑
15.) To have extra phone, computer or game time (Activity) or			❑		
To receive a book or game you can enjoy (Tangible)		❑			
16.) To have your parents tell others how proud they are of you (Adult Approval) or				❑	
To be given your favorite drink, e.g., soft drink, sports drink (Consumable)	❑				

Subtotals: ____ ____ ____ ____ ____

17.) To be given a book or game you can play at home (Tangible) or ☐
To be able to pick a movie to watch at home (Activity ☐
18.) To have your parents tell others how proud they are of you (Adult Approval) or ☐
To be picked by others to be on their team (Peer Approval) ☐
19.) To be given a game you can play at home (Tangible) or ☐
To have your parents tell you that you did something well (Adult Approval) ☐
20.) To have friends ask you to do something with them (Peer Approval) or ☐
To go swimming, play tennis, throw a ball, etc. (Activity) ☐

Previous Page Subtotals: ___ ___ ___ ___ ___

Subtotals: ___ ___ ___ ___ ___

Totals: ___ ___ ___ ___ ___

Motivation	Times Chosen	Ranking in Order of Preference
Tangible Items	_____	_____
Consumable Items	_____	_____
Activity	_____	_____
Adult Approval	_____	_____
Peer Approval	_____	_____

Sample Reinforcers

See Either Home or School Reinforcement Survey for Reinforcers

Daily Reward	Tangibles	Weekly Reward
Silly Putty, Chalk, Balloon		Pokémon Card Set(s),
Comic Book or Coloring Book		Music CD or Music Download Card
New Toy		Jewelry or Game
Coloring Book		Purchase a Board Game

Daily Reward	Consumables	Weekly Reward
Beef Jerky		Select Restaurant
Popcorn		Favorite Meal at home
Cotton Candy		Home Made Ice Cream
Ice Cream Bar		Pizza Party at home with 2-3 friends

Daily Reward	Activities	Weekly Reward
Playing a selected Game at home		Going to Movies with Popcorn and Drink
Pick a TV show or movie that could be watched		Restaurant that has Games
Decide what the family will do on Family night		Ball Machine for Batting or Tennis
Extra phone or computer time		Bowling

Daily Reward	Adult Approval	Weekly Reward
Mom or dad saying you did a great job.		Mom or dad coming to school and showing how proud they are of you
Go bike riding with mom or dad		Going someplace with mom or dad for the evening.
Go for a walk with mom or dad		Spending a day with your parents doing something as a family.

Daily Reward	Peer Approval	Weekly Reward
Playing in the yard with a friend.		Sleep over and you determine what's going to happen
Have a friend over to play computer together.		Being able to take a friend to spend time with at a park, or other location.
Have a friend over just to hang out together.		Spend the night with a friend.

Tangible and Consumable Reinforcers

Sit down with your child, review the Sample Reinforcers and come up with as many reinforcers that you can identify for each area listed below.

Tangibles	
Daily Reward	**Weekly Reward**

Consumables	
Daily Reward	**Weekly Reward**

Activity and Adult Approval Reinforcers

Sit down with your child, review the Sample Reinforcers and come up with as many reinforcers that you can identify for each area listed below.

Activity	
Daily Reward	**Weekly Reward**
Adult Approval	
Daily Reward	**Weekly Reward**

Peer Approval and Other Reinforcers

Sit down with your child, review the Sample Reinforcers and come up with as many reinforcers that you can identify for each area listed below.

Peer Approval	
Daily Reward	Weekly Reward

Any Other Reinforcers	
Daily Reward	Weekly Reward

KIDS UNDER CONSTRUCTION
Structured Disciplinary System

This system was developed to help parents get control of inappropriate behaviors their children may be exhibiting, or if there needs to be a consistent system in place that both parents can follow. It can be used in part or whole to help teach a child appropriate behaviors, appropriate responses to parents, work ethic, self-judgment, self-discipline and ultimately responsibility.

- Kids Under Construction Rules
- Identification of Unacceptable Behaviors – Sample
- Identification of Unacceptable Behaviors Worksheet
- Personal Responsibilities List – Sample
- Personal Responsibilities List Worksheet
- Chore List – Sample
- Chore List Worksheet
- Consequences and their Values – Sample
- Consequences and their Values Worksheet
- Behavior = Consequence Chart – Sample
- Behavior = Consequences Worksheet
- House Rules – Sample
- House Rules Worksheet
- Reward Methods Handout
- The Goal

Kids Under Construction
Rules

Rule 1: Responsibilities must be complete before any money can be earned on other jobs.

- Responsibilities must be completed because you live in the home and should be helping in some way.
- Chores may be completed to make an allowance or to pay for broken or lost items because of a consequence.

Rule 2: If money is owed for consequences, it must be paid before any money goes in your pocket.

Rule 3: If money is owned for anything purchased for you or broken by you, it must be paid before money goes in your pocket

Rule 4: Responsibilities must be completed before you can earn money on a daily basis.

Rule 5: Homework and responsibilities must be completed before free time, or before you can earn money.

Identification of Unacceptable Behaviors

Sample

Instructions:

1. List the behaviors that you want to decrease or stop in the spaces shown below.
2. When finished go back and rate how much each of the behaviors are a problem for you and your child.

1 = No Problem   2 = Mild Problem   3 = Moderate Problem   4 = Significant Problem   5 =Major Problem

Behavioral Concerns	Rating				
	1	2	3	4	5
Throwing things			X		
Destroying things out of anger				X	
Asking for the same thing over and over again				X	
Not listening to me when I tell him to get off the electronic device - doesn't know when to stop					X
Demanding behavior - "You will or else." "Do it now."		X			
Screaming at me		X			
Calling himself names --> Stupid, ugly, fat, an idiot, doesn't deserve to be on this earth		X			
Whining/complaining about getting up and going to camp/school				X	
Refusing to go to school/camp, errands, etc.				X	
Lying to me		X			
Name Calling to parents			X		

Identification of Unacceptable Behaviors

Worksheet

Instructions:

1. List the behaviors that you want to decrease or stop in the spaces shown below.
2. When finished go back and rate how much each of the behaviors are a problem for you and your child.

1 = No Problem   2 = Mild Problem   3 = Moderate Problem   4 = Significant Problem   5 =Major Problem

Behavioral Concerns	Rating				
	1	2	3	4	5

Personal Responsibilities List

Sample

Post in Child's Room
Daily Responsibilities
Make your bed before noon
Put dirty clothes in the hamper
Practice writing daily via homework or summer, pick 5 words and write them correctly
Read a book for 20 minutes daily
Read a book for 20 minutes daily
Get out of bed, finish morning routine (dressed, teeth brushed, breakfast) and in car by 7:30 am
Put clean clothes in drawers or hang them up
Clean bathroom after use, e.g., wipe out sink, pick up clothes, put things back where they belong
Put wet or dirty clothes from bathroom in hamper
Weekly Responsibilities
Bring personal laundry and linens downstairs, sort and stain-treat
Deep Clean Bathroom, e.g., mop, clean toilet, clean sink, clean shower/tub, clean towels
Make bed with clean sheets
Review calendar for coming week and prepare it as needed.
NOTE: You should not give a child many responsibilities. The younger the child the fewer the responsibilities! Two to three responsibilities are usually enough for most children. Three to five for older children.

RESPONSIBILITIES MUST BE COMPLETED BEFORE FREE TIME OR CHORES!!!

Personal Responsibilities List

Worksheet

Post in Child's Room
Daily Responsibilities
Weekly Responsibilities

RESPONSIBILITIES MUST BE COMPLETED BEFORE FREE TIME OR CHORES!!!

Chore List

Sample

Value	CAN EARN UP TO $8 A WEEK (Post to Cork Board)
$0.50	Set the table for dinner
$0.75	Dry and put away dishes
$1.00	Sweep the kitchen/family room floor/vacuum rug
$0.50	Clean off table after dinner and bring all dishes to kitchen
$1.00	Fold towels
$1.50	Wipe down bathroom sink, mirror, toilet
$0.50	Put clothes in drawer/closet
$.50	Load dishwasher
$1.00	Unload the dishwasher and put away what is possible
$2.00	Wash light load of dishes
$0.50	Bring trash to curb
$2.00	Take pet(s) for a walk for at least 15 min
$0.50	Feed and water pet(s)
$5.00	Pull weeds from an entire bed
$3.00	Clean up game room: Garbage thrown away, TV stand dusted, TV screen wiped, floor vacuumed
$3.00	Write a letter to a friend, relative that includes at least 10 sentences. Include something in the letter (picture, rainbow loom bracelet, photograph)
$0.50	Get the mail
$0.50	Water the planters
$1.00	Sweep the outdoor patio that is covered and take to garbage can
$5.00	Wash car (must be done well and approved)
$3.00	Mow lawn front
$3.00	Mow lawn back
$1.00	Fold your laundry/take to your room and put it up
$.75	Mop kitchen floor
$2.00	Deep clean mom and dad's bathroom
$.75	Vacuum or mop one room
$.75	Vacuum/clean stairs and hallways

Chore List

Worksheet

Value	CAN EARN UP TO $_____ A WEEK (Post to Cork Board)

Consequences and Their Values

Sample

Value	Post in Child's Room
$5.00	Losing the Xbox
$3.00	Losing computer privileges
$2.00	Losing an Xbox game
$3.00	Losing iPad
None	Short Time out (consider age—younger should be shorter times)
$3.00	Loss of phone privileges
$2.00	Can't buy from iTunes
$3.00	Losing TV
None	Losing Movie Night at home
$3.00	Disable chat and playing with friends on Xbox
$2.00	Loss of pool privileges
$.1.50	Small Toys
$1-$3 to get back item	Sitting in the middle of the bed for 15 minutes. Homework or reading a book allowed. Anything else that is touched will be taken and must be earned back.
	.

Rule: Any item lost for 24, 48, or 72 hours must be earned back by earning the value of it doing chores. It cannot be paid with money already earned.

Items that Can't be Earned Back—One-time events

	Time Out
	Go to Bed Early
	Loss of Evening Privileges
	Loss of Evening Privileges in room: Evening Grounding: Go to room, sit in middle of bed for evening. Homework or reading a book allowed. Anything else that is touched will be taken and must be earned back.
	Loss of Friday or Saturday evening privileges: Must stay at home. May be able to participate in selected family activities
	Loss of Saturday Night Privileges
	Loss of Weekend privileges
	Loss of weekend privileges—must stay at home. May be able to participate in selected family activities.

Consequences and Their Values
Worksheet

Value	Post in Child's Room
Rule: Any item lost for 24, 48, or 72 hours must be earned back by earning the value of it doing chores. It cannot be paid with money already earned.	

Behavior = Consequence Chart
Sample

Behavior	Consequences
Throwing things	Pick it up and put it back; time out for 10+ minutes
Destroying things out of anger	Anything destroyed he will need to buy back. Go to room (read, homework) for 2-3 hours
Asking for the same thing over and over again	Broken Record
Not listening to me when I tell him to get off the electronic device - doesn't know when to stop	Loses the privilege for 48 hours
Demanding behavior - "You will or else." "Do it now."	10-minute time-out; Add 5 min if he continues to do it. One more time lose Xbox for 1 day
Screaming at me	10-minute time-out.
Calling himself names --> Stupid, ugly, fat, an idiot, doesn't deserve to be on this earth	Get calm and discuss it. "You're capable. I believe in you. You can make good choices."
Whining/complaining about getting up and going to camp/school	Start time to play video games on the weekend gets increased by 1 hour
Refusing to go to school/camp, errands, etc.	Privilege removed for specified # of hours/days. Stay home with no access to technology and stay in room.
Lying to me	I decide how long. Lying produces a trust issue. Consequence will cover that lie plus ones that I didn't catch. All privileges are gone!
Name Calling to parents	15 minutes early to bed or chores before free time
(Post to Cork Board or where Appropriate)	

Behavior = Consequence Chart

Worksheet

Behavior	Consequences
(Post to Cork Board or where Appropriate)	

House Rules

Sample

Post in Child's Room
Free time until dinner (up to 60 min)
No electronic devices during dinner
Finish responsibilities and homework, before free time until time to get ready for bed
If you use something you are not supposed to use, or if you lose a privilege, then you lose that privilege for 48 hours - you will need to earn items lost back through chores.
Xbox gets shut down at 8:00 pm
In bed by 9:00
Must show teacher initialed assignment book to parent each day after school.
Must stay in own room all night.
Summer schedule: all gaming devices shut off at 8:30 pm
School schedule: no Xbox during the school week, iPad and computer games off at 8:00 pm, no gaming on days with sports activities; weekend shut off at 8:30 pm

House Rules

Worksheet

Post in Child's Room

Reward Methods

Handout

Mystery Envelope (Weekly Reward option)	Place a higher level preferred reward in the envelope. Can't see what it is until Friday after school/early evening.
Weekly Treasure Chest	Place higher level preferred rewards (more expensive) in the Treasure Chest. He can pick any reward in the chest if he has had a good week (you must define good week).
Daily Treasure Chest	Place lower level (less expensive) rewards in the Daily Treasure Chest. He can pick any one of the rewards that he chooses just before the end of the day if he had a good day (you must define good day).
Weekly Selective Rewards	Have your child select a higher level weekly reward he wants to work for. This needs to be something special that he is willing to work hard for. This reward should change periodically.
Daily Selective Rewards	Have your child select a less expensive, but desired reward he wants to work for. This needs to be something that he is willing to work hard for on a daily basis. This should change periodically.

The Goal

The ultimate goal of this system is for you to get to a point that it is no longer necessary. Some of the strategies will be beneficial to all parents no matter what the situation. However, the goal should be to get your child to the point that a strong, rigid parent system is not necessary. The more your child learns responsibility, the more he internalizes good self-judgment and self-discipline, the less you will need this system.

Use this system until your child shows that he is consistently making right choice. When that occurs, you can back off a bit. He may not even notice that you are using the system less simply because it is not needed.

Until then maintain the system. You will be:

- Holding him accountable for his actions.
- Teaching him good self-judgment. He will clearly learn right from wrong.
- Teaching him good self-discipline. He will begin the process of making right choices most of the time.
- Letting him know that privileges are earned not deserved.
- Teaching him that money is earned not given, and in process you will be teaching him a better work ethic that will help him for the rest of his life.
- Teaching him that personal responsibilities and work (school) come before play or personal wants or desires.
- Teaching him respect for those in authority, whether it be parents, teachers or bosses later in life.
- Teaching him that there are natural rewards for doing the right thing. People will respect him. People will like being around him. He will begin to understand that he is truly a good person with good values. As a result, he will have a good, healthy self-image.
- Ultimately teaching him that he is not entitled. He doesn't get things, have privileges without putting any work into it, without making good choices.
- Showing him love, because love has the best interests of the receiver in mind.

When he has internalized these things, he will have a good chance of becoming a healthy, productive and successful adult that you can be proud of. However, for him to do this you must help him learn and utilize the things shown above until he internalizes them. That's your job. That's how you can love your child in ways that will help him throughout the rest of his life.

Appendix

Using EIAG After a Poor Choice

Exploring is one of the most important tools you can use to help a child learn how to make better choices in the future. After the event, after the consequence and after your child has calmed down take a moment and do EIAG. All inappropriate behavior can be used as an opportunity to teach your child more appropriate behavior. When you ask the What? Why? and How? questions you are helping your child clarify what is right, what is wrong and how he can handle things better in the future. Make copies of this worksheet. You can use it over and over as you help your child learn how to identify better choices.

E.I.A.G.: EXPERIENCE-IDENTIFY-ANALYZE-GENERALIZE		
Steps	Questions to Ask	Personal Example
Experience:	Something Happens	
Identify:	Ask: "What happened?" "What are you feeling?" "What did you see?"	
Analyze:	Ask: "Why was that significant?" "What caused that to happen?" "Why did it happen to you?" "What made that important?"	
Generalize:	Ask: "How can you use this?" "How could you do it differently next time?" "What did you learn from the experience?"	

Adapted from Steven Glenn's work entitled, Raising Self-Reliant Children in a Self-Indulgent World.

References and Recommended Readings

Bandura, A. **Principles of Behavior Modification**, Holt, Reinhart & Winston , New York , 1969.

Baumrind, Diana PhD Effects of Authoritative Parental Control on Child Behavior, Univ. of CA at Berkeley research paper.

Crites, Jr. F. Russell **Assertiveness, Boundaries and Conflict Management workbook - Revised.** Dallas, TX: CPC, 2016.

Crites, Jr. F. Russell **Family Therapy Manual: A Pragmatic Approach to Addressing Dysfunctional Family Issues – Revised.** Dallas, TX: CPC, 2016.

Crites, Jr. F. Russell **The Responsibility Factor: High Risk vs Low Risk Parenting.** Being Revised.

Dobson, James **The Strong Willed Child-Revised.** New York, NY.: Tyndale Momentum, 2004.

Gershoff, E.T. (2002a) "Corporal punishment by parents and associated child behaviors and experiences: A meta-analytic and theoretical review" Psychological Bulletin, 128(4):539–579.

Glenn, H. Stephen **Raising Self-Reliant Children in a Self-Indulgent World.** Roseville, CA.: Prima Publications, 2000.

Kochanska, G., K.C. Coy and K.T. Murray (2001) "The development of self-regulation in the first four years of life" Child Development, 72(4):1091–1111.

Larzelere RE, Schneider WN, Larson DB, Pike PL. The effects of discipline responses in delaying toddler misbehavior recurrences. Child & Family Behavior Therapy 1996;18:35-57.

Larzelere RE, Sather PR, Schneider WN, Larson DB, Pike PL. Punishment enhances reasoning's effectiveness as a disciplinary response to toddlers. Journal of Marriage and the Family 1998;60:388-403.

Wissow, L.S. (2002) "Child discipline in the first three years of life" in N. Halfon, K.T. McLearn and M.A. Schuster (eds.) Child Rearing in America: Challenges Facing Parents with Young Children, Cambridge University Press, New York (pp.146–177).

Other Works by this Author

NOTE: If you want to order any of the works show below go to: amazon.com/author/russcrites There is a list of most of the books, workbooks and manuals he has authored.

Adult Child Therapy Manual: Counseling Individuals who come from Dysfunctional Families - Revised. This 200 plus page manual includes forms and therapy aids, diagnostic tools, how to identify and resolve family of origin issues, addresses adult child issues, show you how to identify and resolve codependency issues, how to deal with past issues, how to change thinking and habits, and how visualizations, affirmations other methods that will help your client experience positive change and more. This manual will soon be on Amazon. It is currently being revised. Watch for it on Amazon!

Adult Child Therapy Workbook: This workbook included the Adult Child Assessment which measures over thirty adult child characteristics that can cause individuals difficulties. There are worksheets for each of the characteristics identified in the assessment as well as many helpful strategies. This workbook is available on Amazon!

Assertiveness, Boundaries and Conflict Management – Revised Workbook. This workbook will soon be available on Amazon.

Bipolar or ADHD: Educational and Home Based Strategies for Bipolar Disorder, ADHD and other Co-Existing Conditions. This book covers the different types of bipolar disorder, strategies for elementary and secondary students, how to reduce mood swings and rage states, how to teach students to self-monitor, and a disciplinary model for home and school. It also addresses ADHD, Anxiety, Depression, Oppositional Defiant, Conduct Disorder and more. Strategies to address these issues are also included. This book is available on Amazon or through your local bookstore.

Coping Styles Assessment which measures Family of Origin Roles, Codependency's, Unhealthy Communication Styles, Unhealthy Family Rules, three underlying motivations, and over 30 Adult Child characteristics. It also provides a four point code depending on the issues identified and the underlying motivations that the person is experiencing. There are sixteen different individualized CODE workbooks that can be purchased so that a person can work through multiple issues personally, or with a therapists help and guidance. This test can be purchased by contacting the author. You may also obtain the **Coping Styles Assessment Quick Check** at no expense by going to www.critescounseling.com. Click the **Books and Materials** Tab. Look at the very bottom of the page for a file entitled, **Coping Styles Quick Check**. Download this file, complete the assessment and determine your code. This may be used by therapists to obtain codes for workbook.

CODE books for the Coping Styles Assessment. There are sixteen different CODE books available and are based on the data obtained from the **Coping Styles Assessment,** or the **Coping Styles Quick Check** assessment. The code books address the following issues: 1) Nine Family of Origin Roles, 2) Twelve Family of Origin Rules in both past and present families, 3) Twelve Codependency Roles, 4) Four Unhealthy Communication Styles, 5) Three Underlying Motivations (Self-Oriented Control, Other Oriented Accommodation, and Avoidance), 6) Neglect and Abuse Issues, 7) Control Issues and more depending on the code. It also addresses the unique concept of Bipolar Codependency for those who scores suggest it is an issue. The following codes are possible: HBOA, HBON, HUOA, HUON, HBSA, HBSN, HUSA, HUSN, RBOA, RBON, RUOA, RUON, RBSA, RBSN, RUSA, RUSN. These workbooks are on Amazon.

Depression and Anxiety in Students: Strategies for Counselors and Teachers. This is a power packed strategy guide that both counselors and teachers can use to positively impact students who have depression or anxiety. Different types of anxiety are addressed. This strategy guide is available on Amazon.

Executive Function Disorder: Educational/Behavioral Strategies for ADHD, Bipolar, Asperger and other Brain Based Disorders. This book addresses the identification of over ten brain based issues that cause difficulties for students. It includes strategies for home and school for Planning, Prioritizing, Time Management, Organization of Materials, Organization of Space, Activating to Work, Processing Speed, Self-Monitoring, Shifting, Emotional Control, Working Memory and more. This book is available on Amazon or through your local bookstore.

Family Therapy Manual: A Pragmatic Approach to Addressing Dysfunctional Family Issues – Revised. This 200 plus page manual includes Assessment tools for working with families, forms and therapy aids, information on Dysfunctional Family Roles, Strategies to Promote a Healthy Family, Promoting Healthy Family Traits, Dysfunctional Family Rules, Teaching Values and Parenting, Discipline and more. This manual will soon be on Amazon. It is currently being revised. Watch for it on Amazon!

Foundations Workbook – Revised. This workbook assists the person as he attempts to identify a healthy sense of self. Mental, Social, Physical and Spiritual/Moral and Emotional aspects of self are addressed. Strategies to improve in all areas are provided. Foundations, which is core in the Genesis System for Self-Improvement, is also discussed in detail. Foundations includes sections on how to take your mind back. You will learn how to control what you think and when you think it instead of having your mind run amuck and produce chaos, anxiety and frustration. Next, Foundations teaches you the strategies necessary for you to reprogram your unconscious mind. Unhealthy imbedded beliefs often control what you think, say and do. You will learn how to change these unhealthy imbedded beliefs so that your mind will direct you toward new healthier thoughts, words and actions. To help with this a method called the Inner Sanctum is discussed and taught. Using the Inner Sanctum you can begin to produce change at a deeper more powerful way. This workbook is available on Amazon

Kids Under Construction: Help for the Strong-Willed Child Workbook. This workbook is for parents who have children who are out of control. The primary intent of this work is to help you identify strategies and a system that will help you better control a child who is out of control in some way. Your child might be oppositional, have conduct issues or he may simply be very strong willed. Regardless of the issue your child has, this work provides tools that will help you manage his behavior in an easier more effective way. This workbook is available on Amazon.

Marriage Go Round: The First Journey – A Therapeutic Guide for Helping Couples Heal and Rekindle Love in Their Lives. This manual includes forms and therapy aids, what to do when only one partner comes to therapy, a discussion of relationship cycles, identifies and discusses the stages of relationship, addresses the necessity for change, conflict resolution or management, forgiveness and reconciliation, how to reactivate an individual's emotional core, three foundational pillars (Commitment, Partner being a Priority, Service). Eight specific issues are addressed in this manual. However, thirty-two specific love expectations are identified using the Marriage Go Round Assessment. These thirty-two different expectations are assessed and prioritized for each person in the relationship. Some of the areas addressed are Trust, Romance, Physical Affection, Admiration, Having Fun, Emotional Connection, Finances, Communication, Appreciation, Honesty, personal Space, Respect, Spiritual Unity, Sexuality and Sexual Affection. Worksheets, strategies, handouts, individual and couple exercises are all part of the system. This Manual is available on Amazon or through your local bookstore.

Marriage Go Round: The Second Journey: This manual has over 300 plus pages of worksheets, strategies, handouts, individual and couple exercises are all part of the system. While the first manual covers some basic foundational material, The Second Journey covers the twenty-four remaining love expectations. It also provides additional strategies or information for issues identified in the First Journey. This manual will soon be available on Amazon or through your local bookstore. It is currently being completed.

Marriage Go Round Basic Workbook: Nine Steps to Improving Your Relationship and Rekindling Love in Your life. This is the companion workbook that clients can use in a therapy situation. Therapists may purchase multiple copies at a discount through the author, or can buy them individually through Amazon. This workbook is available for anyone through Amazon or a local bookstore.

The Responsibility Factor: High Risk vs Low Risk Parenting. This book identifies specific high risk activities or parenting styles that can contribute to long lasting issues for a child. It also identifies how parents can implement strategies and systems in the home that will help a child develop good self-judgment, self-discipline and responsibility. Being revised.

Three Faces of Codependency: This is the foundational book that communicates the underlying principles of the Genesis System. It reviews the three types of codependencies with their underlying motivations. It will also help you understand how codependency can negatively impact you on a day by day basis. This book is available for anyone through Amazon or may be ordered from your local bookstore.

Twelve Step Workbook – Revised: This particular workbook addresses the twelve steps that may be taken to help you heal more efficiently. The steps are broken down to show whether or not there is an internal, an external element to each step. Some steps actually require both an internal and external response. Regardless, this work is extremely practical and provides helpful worksheets that can be used over and over again as needed. This work also includes a segment entitled Foundations. Foundations is a core element of the Genesis System for Self-Improvement. Foundations teaches you the strategies necessary for you to reprogram your unconscious mind. Unhealthy embedded beliefs often control what you think, say and do. You will learn how to change these unhealthy embedded beliefs so that your mind will direct you toward new healthier thoughts, words and actions. To help with this a method called the Inner Sanctum is discussed and taught. Using the Inner Sanctum you can begin to produce change at a deeper more powerful way. This workbook is available on Amazon or through your local bookstore.

NOTE: Most of these books, manuals and workbooks can be purchased through Amazon or your local book store. Workbooks can be purchased at a discount for therapists who wish to resell them for therapy use. Call author for more information.

SEMINAR INFORMATION

Anyone interested in hosting a training seminar for the Genesis System for dealing with personal issues and codependency or any other program specific to the materials listed above please contact:

F. Russell Crites, M.S., LPC, LMFT, LSSP, NBCCH, CPC
Crites Counseling and Consultation
106 N. Denton Tap Rd. Ste 210-216
Coppell, Texas 75019
www.critescounseling.com
amazon.com/author/russcrites
972-506-7111

Please report any copyright violations to 972-506-7111. Orders can also be obtained by calling 972-506-7111 or by going to Amazon.com. Orders of five or more workbooks at a time from the author get a 30% discount and can be resold for client use.